Word 365 Lists

EASY WORD 365 ESSENTIALS - BOOK 3

M.L. HUMPHREY

SELECT TITLES BY M.L. HUMPHREY

WORD 365 ESSENTIALS
Word 365 for Beginners
Intermediate Word 365

EASY WORD 365 ESSENTIALS
Text Formatting
Page Formatting
Lists
Tables
Styles and Breaks
Track Changes

See mlhumphrey.com for more Microsoft Office titles

CONTENTS

Introduction

This book is part of the *Easy Word 365 Essentials* series of titles. These are targeted titles that are excerpted from the main *Word 365 Essentials* series and are focused on one specific topic.

If you want a more general introduction to Word, then you should check out the *Word 365 Essentials* titles instead. In this case, start with *Word 365 for Beginners* which covers bulleted and numbered lists as well as other introductory topics.

But if all you want to learn is bulleted, numbered, and multilevel lists, then this is the book for you.

Bulleted Lists

Chances are that if you write enough corporate reports, at some point in time you will be asked to either create a bulleted list or a numbered list, so we're going to cover those now.

A bulleted list takes a series of text entries on different rows and puts bullet points in front of them. Like this:

- This is my first point
- This is my second one
- This is my third one and it's a real doozy.
- This is my fourth point.

Note that it indents those entries by default.

To apply bullets to a list, select your text and then go to the top row of the Paragraph section of the Home tab and click on the Bullets image. That will apply a standard bulleted list like you see above.

If you instead click on the dropdown arrow there, you can choose the type of bullet to use:

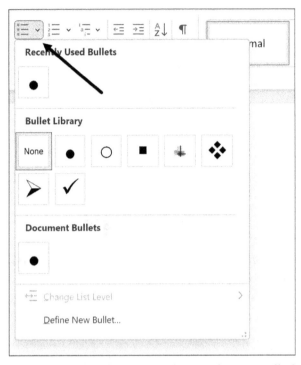

Because I just applied a bulleted list, I have a section at the top called Recently Used Bullets that shows the type of bullet I just used. Below that is the full list of bullets that you can choose from by default under the heading Bullet Library. And below that is a listing of any bullet types used in this particular document.

You can also click on that Define New Bullet option at the bottom to create a brand-new bullet type, but we're not going to do that here.

It's pretty basic to create a bulleted list.

Once a line of text is bulleted, when you hit enter from that line, the next line will also be bulleted.

You can remove that bullet by using the Backspace key, but you will still be indented to align with the text entry in the line above. If you Backspace two more times that should take you to the left-hand side of the page.

Another option is to hit Enter twice from a bulleted line. That will also remove the bullet point and take you back to the left-hand side of the page.

With bulleted lists the continuity of the list isn't an issue the way it is with numbered lists. But if you start adjusting the indent of various lines and are using bullets in multiple locations in your document you can end up with a situation where the appearance of a bulleted list on one page does not match that on another. So be careful if you go down that road.

Also, if you start a bulleted list and then have indented bullets, those indented bullets will be different by default. Like so:

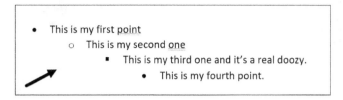

- This is my first point
  - This is my second one
    - This is my third one and it's a real doozy.
      - This is my fourth point.

Word does this automatically as you indent each level and will automatically apply that bullet consistently for that indent level. Note that it cycled back to the first bullet type when I reached the fourth level.

You can customize this, too, using the Bullets dropdown, but exercise caution when doing so.

I indented each line there using the Tab key after clicking in front of the first letter of each row, but you can also go back to the Bullets dropdown and use the Change List Level secondary menu to choose an indent level for each line.

Shift + Tab will reverse the text one indent level.

You can also use the Decrease and Increase Indent options in the Paragraph section of the Home tab. The advantage of using those is that you can click anywhere on that line of text, you don't have to click at the start of the line like you do when using Tab or Shift + Tab.

To remove bullets from a bulleted list, select your list and then click on the bulleted list option again.

The mini formatting menu also includes the Bullets dropdown menu.

Numbered Lists

At their most basic, numbered lists work much the same way as bulleted lists. Select your rows of text and then click on the Numbering option in the top row of the Paragraph section of the Home tab. Word will turn your entries into a numbered list that looks like this:

1. This is my first point
2. This is my second one
3. This is my third one and it's a real doozy.
4. This is my fourth point.

Note that the numbered list is indented by default.

You can also start a numbered list by simply typing the first entry (1., A., etc.) and Word will convert that into a numbered list for you. (If you don't want that, just use Undo, Ctrl + X, right away.)

If you hit enter from a line that's a numbered entry it will either continue the numbering (if at the bottom of the list) or insert a new numbered entry and then renumber all other entries in the list (if in the midst of a numbered list).

You can remove a numbered entry using the Backspace key. When you do that, like I have below with what would have been number 2 in this list, Word will renumber any subsequent numbered entries to maintain a numbered list that goes from 1 to 2 to 3, etc.

1. This is my first point

2. This is my second one
3. This is my third one and it's a real doozy.
4. This is my fourth point.

There is a Numbering dropdown menu that lets you choose other numbering styles:

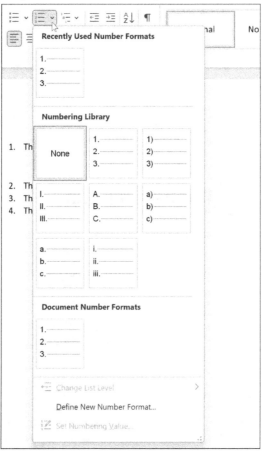

If you click on one of your numbered entries and then choose a different format from that dropdown it will change all of your entries to the new format.

Select the Set Numbering Value option at the bottom of that dropdown menu to open the Set Numbering dialogue box:

This dialogue box allows you to start a new numbered list instead of continuing the prior one or to continue a numbered list from earlier in the document. You can also choose the value for that entry.

To create a multi-level list using the Numbering option, use Tab or the Indent option to move the text to that next level. Word will automatically assign a numbering option for that next level.

Here you can see it went 1, a, i, and then back to 1 again.

```
1. This is my first item.
      a. And here's my subpoint
      b. And another one
             i. And then a sub-subpoint
            ii. And another one
                   1. And then another
```

When I changed the first level to an A. instead, it still went with a, i, and then 1 for the next three levels. So it doesn't follow the standard format for an outline that I was taught in school.

If you really need to go down that route, the Multilevel List option will give you far more control, but we're not covering it here because it can be very finicky in my experience.

Also, be very, very careful using either multiple numbered lists in a large document or using numbered lists where there are large gaps between the entries.

It's possible to do and I have certainly done so more than once. But this is one of those areas where I have wasted more time and energy than I can count going back and forth between different sections of a document to make sure that a change on page 10 didn't renumber my entries on page 65 or vice versa.

This may be more of an issue with Multilevel Lists, but it's definitely something to watch for. At the very end, when you are done making all other edits, if you are using numbered lists, make sure that you walk through your document from start to finish to confirm that all of the lists are working as expected.

To remove numbering, select your entries and then click on the numbering option once more.

The mini formatting menu also includes a Numbering dropdown menu.

MultiLevel Lists

Time for one of the most annoying topics I wanted to cover in this book, multilevel lists.

Why are they so annoying? If you use them as-is and for the entire document, they're not. But if you try to customize them it can be very painful. Same with if you try to use them in addition to other lists in the same document.

Also, last I checked, they need customization because they don't follow a standard format. The one I'm going to show you here, for example, is fine for the first three levels, but then uses an a with a paren instead of an a with a period, which is not how I was taught it should go.

But let's go look, shall we.

Multilevel lists can be found in the Paragraph section of the Home tab in the top row next to bulleted lists and numbered lists which were already covered in *Word 365 for Beginner*s:

The list choice that's closest to what I was raised with in school is that third one down on the left in the list library, so I'm going to select it and then create a few entries.

Here's what I came up with:

> I. This is the main level entry for this <u>topic</u>
> **This is me adding text below that point.**
>
> A. Now I want a sub-entry.
> B. And another sub-entry.
> ◀ 1. And a subpoint of that one.

A few points to mention here that are important.

With a bulleted or numbered list, when you hit Enter the next line is automatically also bulleted or numbered. With a multilevel list, that is not the case. The next line is text.

Furthermore, that text is not indented. The cursor goes back each time to the far left-hand side of the page.

Using the Tab key will get you to a point directly below the text in the prior line so you can add a description or paragraph like I did above under the first main point.

For those other entries, the A, the B, and the 1, I had to go up to the Paragraph section of the Home tab, click on the dropdown for Multilevel List, and then click on the current list I was using.

If your cursor is not already indented to the level you want, place the cursor before the text in that line and use the Tab key to move the text one indent level at a time.

Another option for getting the right list level is to go back to that dropdown and use the Change List Level option to choose the desired list level.

You can also use the Indent options in the Paragraph section of the Home tab.

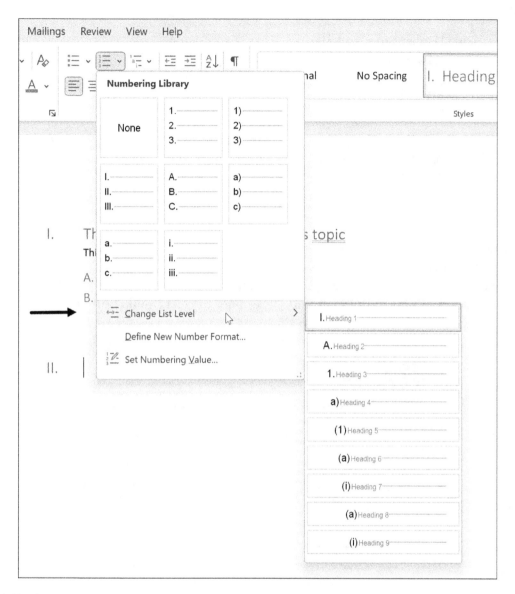

Each list level will have a black arrow that will appear to the left of the entry when you hold your mouse over it that you can click on to hide everything below that entry.

The nice thing about the multilevel list is that it does continue throughout your document even if there is text in between. So if I type text and then add a new multilevel list entry after that text, it will continue the numbering from above:

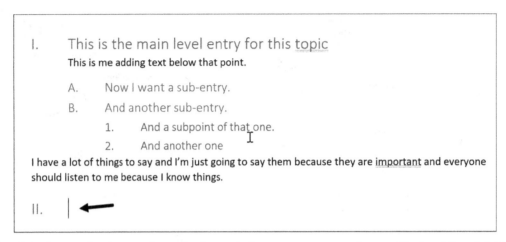

If the default numbering options don't work for you, you can choose Define New Multilevel List from the multilevel list dropdown to create your own list. That will open the Define New Multilevel List dialogue box where you can then for each level choose the number formatting to use, the alignment for the number, and the amount the text should be indented.

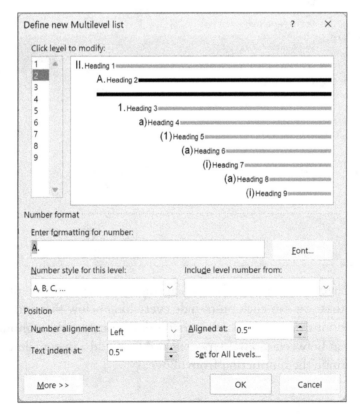

Click on More to see more options such as how to separate the number from the text (default is a Tab character) and where to apply those changes and what numbering to start at and when to restart that level's numbering.

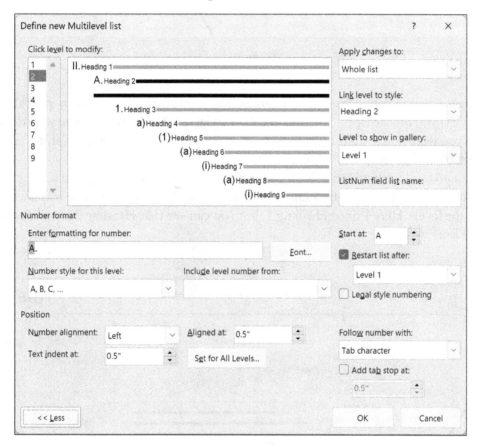

These list entries are tied into the Heading 1, Heading 2, etc. styles, which can be problematic. When I tried to add an entry using a multilevel list to the very end of an existing document that was already using Heading 1 for the chapter headers, Word automatically converted all of my prior chapter headers to parts of the multilevel list I'd just added.

You can see here that Heading 1 and Heading 2 now are formatted to be part of a multilevel list.

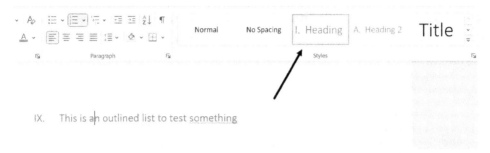

IX.   This is an outlined list to test something

Which, hey if you're using that outline format for your entire document, is probably great, because it lets you quickly apply the multilevel list styles as needed as you write your document.

But if you were doing what I just tried to do, which is use a multilevel list at the end of the document, it's a disaster.

You can go back to that Define New Multilevel List option and change the setting that links the first level of the list to the Heading 1 style and click OK to fix that. But you need to do it for all of the levels. Here I fixed Heading 1, but you can see that Heading 2 is still tied into the multilevel list:

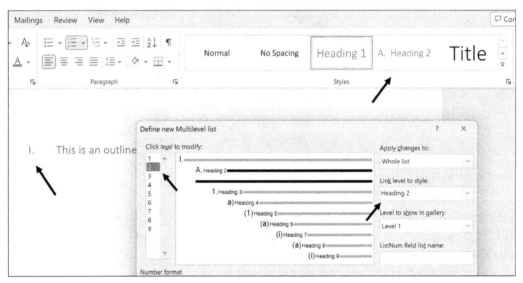

My advice to you if you want to use the multilevel list option is to make sure that your entire document uses the list and that there are no other Heading styles or other numbered or bulleted lists in the document.

Also, if you are trying to fix a document that has a multilevel list that isn't working properly, you may have to create that multilevel list in a new document and then paste in your text one paragraph at a time to fix it. (Hopefully not, but that is what I have had to do once or twice when nothing else would work.)

Not the best use of time, but it may be the only way to get it all to work the way it should.

Appendix A: Basic Terminology Recap

These terms were covered in detail in *Word 365 for Beginners*. This is just meant as a refresher.

Tab

When I refer to a tab, I am referring to the menu options at the top of the screen. The tab options that are available by default are File, Home, Insert, Draw, Design, Layout, References, Mailings, Review, View, and Help, but for certain tasks additional tabs will appear.

Click

If I tell you to click on something, that means to move your cursor over to that location and then either right-click or left-click. If I don't say which to do, left-click.

Left-Click / Right-Click

A left-click is generally for selecting something and involves using the left-hand side of your mouse or bottom left-hand corner of your trackpad. A right-click is generally for opening a dropdown menu and involves using the right-hand side of your mouse or bottom right-hand corner of your trackpad.

Left-Click and Drag

Left-click and drag means to left-click and then hold that left-click as you move your mouse.

Dropdown Menu

A dropdown menu is a list of choices that you can view by right-clicking in a specific spot or clicking on an arrow next to or below one of the available choices under the tabs up top. Depending on where you are in the workspace, a dropdown menu may actually drop upward from that spot.

Expansion Arrow

In the bottom right corner of some of the sections under the tabs in the top menu you will see an arrow, which I refer to as an expansion arrow. Clicking on an expansion arrow will usually open a dialogue box or task pane and is often the way to see the largest number of options.

Dialogue Box

A dialogue box is a pop-up box that will open on top of your workspace and will usually include the largest number of choices for that particular setting or task.

Scroll Bar

Scroll bars appear when there are more options than can appear on the screen or when your document is longer than will show on the screen. They can be used to move through the remainder of the choices or document.

Task Pane

A task pane is a set of additional options that will appear to the sides or even below the main workspace. The Navigation pane is by default visible on the left-hand side of the workspace. You can close a task pane by clicking on the X in the top right corner of the pane.

Control Shortcuts

Control shortcuts are shortcuts that let you perform certain tasks in Word. I will write them as Ctrl + and then a character. That means to hold down both the Ctrl key and that character. So Ctrl + C means hold down Ctrl and C, which will let you copy your selection. Even though I will write each shortcut using a capital letter it doesn't have to be the capitalized version to work.

About the Author

M.L. Humphrey is a former stockbroker with a degree in Economics from Stanford and an MBA from Wharton who has spent close to twenty years as a regulator and consultant in the financial services industry.

You can reach M.L. at mlhumphreywriter@gmail.com or at mlhumphrey.com.

www.ingramcontent.com/pod-product-compliance
Lightning Source LLC
Chambersburg PA
CBHW060515060326
40689CB00020B/4752